THE
YOUNG
ENTREPRENEUR
Academy

START YOUR OWN BUSINESS AT ANY AGE!

Second Edition
2025

Written by

Laina J. Brickley

Published by Brick x Brick Consulting, LLC

ISBN: 979-8-218-33573-1

To Carter and Ava for your inspiration and Andrew for your unwavering love and support.

TABLE OF
CONTENTS

WHERE BIG IDEAS BEGIN
WELCOME FUTURE CEO

Hey future CEOs!

Are you ready to turn your ideas into something awesome? At The Young Entrepreneur Academy, we're going to help you use your creativity, learn real business skills, and build something that's totally your own.

What Is The Young Entrepreneur Academy?

It's a fun and exciting program made just for kids and teens who want to explore the world of entrepreneurship—that means starting and running your own business!

You'll get to:

- Think up cool business ideas
- Do hands-on projects and fun activities
- Learn how to sell your product or service
- Discover what it takes to be a great leader

Whether you dream of opening a slime shop, designing clothing, selling snacks, or inventing the next big thing, you're in the right place!

Why Start Now?

You don't have to wait until you're an adult to start a business. Learning how to be an entrepreneur while you're young:

- Builds confidence
- Teaches problem-solving and money skills
- Helps you turn your passions into profits

And best of all—it's fun!

At The Young Entrepreneur Academy, we believe in you. We're here to help you learn, grow, and bring your ideas to life. You've got the talent—now let's help you turn it into something amazing.

IDEAS:

STEP ONE:
CHOOSE A BUSINESS IDEA

Complete Pages 5 - 19

Discover What You're Good At (and What You Love!)

Starting a business can be an amazing way to turn something you love into something you can share—and even make money from! But before you pick a business idea, it helps to first understand you.

That's where the What I Love To Do and What I'm Good At worksheets comes in!

These simple worksheets do exactly what they think they do, they help you think about:

- What you're good at
- What you enjoy doing
- What makes you excited to learn more

Once you know these things, you'll have a better idea of what kind of business would be a great fit for you.

Why This Step Is So Important

1. Learn More About Yourself

The worksheet helps you think about your hobbies, talents, and interests.

Example: Do you love drawing? Solving puzzles? Baking? Fixing things?

2. Do What You Love

When you build a business around something you enjoy, you're more likely to stick with it—and have fun doing it!

Example: If you love animals, a dog-walking or a pet-treat business might be perfect for you.

3. Use Your Strengths

Everyone has unique skills! Maybe you're great at making people laugh or really good at organizing. These strengths can become superpowers in your business.

5-Minute Activity: Make a list of 5 things you're good at. Ask a friend or family member to add 3 more they've noticed in you.

4. Spot Cool Business Ideas

When you look at your hobbies and skills all together, you might come up with ideas you hadn't thought of before!

Example: If you like painting AND helping others, you could start a "custom sign" business for birthday parties or school events.

5. Be Happy With Your Work

The best businesses are the ones that feel good to run. When you enjoy what you're doing, your business doesn't just make money—it makes you proud.

Activity: Complete the "What I Love To Do" and "What I'm Good At" worksheets on the next pages

- List your favorite hobbies
- Write down things you're great at
- Think about what people often ask you for help with
- Circle anything that could be turned into a business

Before you sell anything, take time to get to know yourself. The better you understand your talents and interests, the better your business idea will be.

Are you ready to discover the business that's already inside you? Let's start with the worksheet and see where your skills and passions can take you!

WHAT DO I LOVE TO DO?

Instructions: Let's Talk About What You Love to Do!

- Think about your favorite things to do. What makes you excited? Do you enjoy baking cookies, drawing cartoons, playing basketball, dancing, or making videos. Write down anything you love spending time on.

- Be honest!

This is all about YOU. Don't write what you think sounds good—write what you actually enjoy. The best business ideas come from doing what you truly like!

I really love to.......

1.

2.

3.

4.

5.

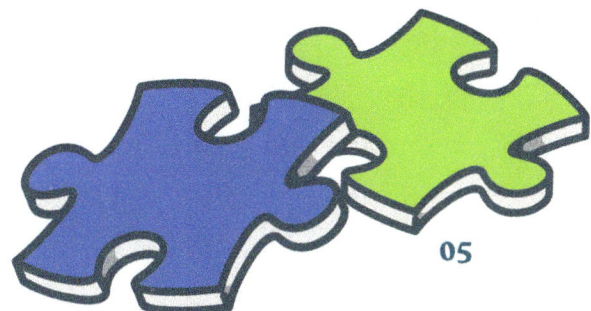

WHAT AM I GOOD AT?

Instructions

1. Think about what you are good at doing. Do you make the best chocolate chip cookies? Are you good at sewing? Is your room perfectly organized? Did you win the school's essay writing contest? Write down at least 5 things you are good at doing below.

2. By writing down what you are good at it will help you figure out what you love to do and what you are talented at doing. This can help you when you brainstorm what kind of business you would enjoy doing.

I'm really good at.......

1.

2.

3.

4.

5.

WHAT I LIKE TO DO + WHAT AM I GOOD AT = A GREAT BUSINESS IDEA!!

Now, let's see how your skills and interests can work together. Write down any combinations or connections you notice between what you like to do and what you are good at doing.

Do you like to bake and you make the best chocolate chip cookies? Maybe you should open a cookie bakery. Do you love to exercise and you are good at teaching people new skills? Maybe you should be a personal trainer or a coach. Do you love to organize and you are good at good at putting together outfits or packing for trips? Maybe you could be a home organizer or a stylist.

Thinking about what you like to do and what you are good at doing will help you make a decision on what might be a good business for you to start.

1. Based on what you like to do and what you are good at doing, what business ideas or activities do you think would be the most fun?

2. Do you like working on group projects? When you work on group projects, how do you help your group complete a project?

4. How can your interests (what you like to do) and skills (what you are good at doing) help you become a successful young entrepreneur?

BUSINESS BRAINSTORMING

Now that you've thought about what you like to do and what you are good at doing, it's time to do some business brainstorming. Brainstorming will help you get all of your ideas out of your head and onto paper. This will help you narrow down and get a clear idea of what you want to do for your future business.

First, you must decide if you are offering a product or a service. Do you want to sell cookies or paintings? Then you are going to start a product business. Are you going to be a personal trainer or give music lessons? If so, you would be starting a service business. Once you decide whether you are starting a service or product business, complete either the Product Brainstorming or Service Brainstorming worksheet. If you are still trying to decide between a few businesses, don't worry; there are extra worksheets to help you work through your ideas so you can narrow them down.

These worksheets are your guide to shaping your entrepreneurial vision. Take your time, be creative, and let your passion shine through.

Instructions:

1. Think about the different product and service businesses you could start.

2. Use this worksheet on <u>page 9</u> to brainstorm your service business or jump forward to <u>page 13</u> if you are planning to start a product business. There are extra brainstorming sheets, so don't worry - there is plenty of room to write down your ideas!

3. Be creative and think outside the box!

4. Consider what you like to do, what you're good at doing, and what services or products you believe people would like to purchase.

SERVICE BUSINESS BRAINSTORMING

Are you planning to start a service-based business? Let's map out your awesome idea step by step!

What kind of service will you offer? (Service Description)

Will you mow lawns, walk dogs, babysit, tutor, clean, or something else?
Write a few sentences explaining what your service is and what problem it helps solve.

Example: I want to offer pet-sitting services for people who are going on vacation. This helps pet owners know their animals are safe and happy while they're away.

Who's It For? (Target Audience)

Who are the people who would want or need your service? Describe your perfect customer.

Example: My ideal customers are busy families who have pets and need someone to care for them after school or on weekends.

What Are You Good At? (Skills Needed)

What skills do you already have that will help you do this job well?
Think about things you've learned at school, at home, or just by doing.

Example: I love animals, I'm responsible, and I already help take care of my own dog.

What Do You Need? (Materials or Resources)

List anything you'll need to get started. This could be tools, supplies, or even help from an adult.

Example: I'll need a leash, water bowls, treats, and a notebook to track appointments.

What Makes You Stand Out? (Unique Selling Point)

What's something special about your service? Why should someone choose you instead of someone else?

Example: I'll leave a thank-you note and a photo of their pet after each visit so the owner feels connected!

EXTRA
SERVICE BUSINESS BRAINSTORMING

What kind of service will you offer? (Service Description)

Will you mow lawns, walk dogs, babysit, tutor, clean, or something else?
Write a few sentences explaining what your service is and what problem it helps solve.

Example: I want to offer pet-sitting services for people who are going on vacation. This helps pet owners know their animals are safe and happy while they're away.

Who's It For? (Target Audience)

Who are the people who would want or need your service? Describe your perfect customer.

Example: My ideal customers are busy families who have pets and need someone to care for them after school or on weekends.

What Are You Good At? (Skills Needed)

What skills do you already have that will help you do this job well?
Think about things you've learned at school, at home, or just by doing.

Example: I love animals, I'm responsible, and I already help take care of my own dog.

What Do You Need? (Materials or Resources)

List anything you'll need to get started. This could be tools, supplies, or even help from an adult.

Example: I'll need a leash, water bowls, treats, and a notebook to track appointments.

What Makes You Stand Out? (Unique Selling Point)

What's something special about your service? Why should someone choose you instead of someone else?

Example: I'll leave a thank-you note and a photo of their pet after each visit so the owner feels connected!

PRODUCT BUSINESS BRAINSTORMING

Are you thinking about selling a product? Use this worksheet to help you plan it out!

What Are You Selling? (Product Description)

Describe the product you want to create or sell. What does it do, and how does it help or make someone's life better?

Example: I want to sell homemade bath bombs that help people relax after a long day. .

Who Would Buy It? (Target Audience)

Who would love your product? Describe your ideal customer—their age, interests, and why they'd want what you're selling.

Example: My perfect customers are kids and teens who like fun self-care products or parents buying gifts.

What Are You Good At? (Skills Needed)

What talents or knowledge do you already have that will help you make and sell this product?

Example: I like crafting, I've made bath bombs before, and I'm good at decorating things to make them look nice.

What Will You Need? (Materials or Resources)

Make a list of supplies, tools, or other things you'll need to create your product.

Example: I'll need baking soda, essential oils, molds, packaging, and labels.

What Makes It Special? (Unique Selling Point)

What makes your product stand out from others? Why would someone choose your product over another?

Example: My bath bombs are made with natural ingredients and come with a surprise charm inside!

EXTRA
PRODUCT BUSINESS BRAINSTORMING

What Are You Selling? (Product Description)

Describe the product you want to create or sell. What does it do, and how does it help or make someone's life better?

Example: I want to sell homemade bath bombs that help people relax after a long day.

Who Would Buy It? (Target Audience)

Who would love your product? Describe your ideal customer—their age, interests, and why they'd want what you're selling.

Example: My perfect customers are kids and teens who like fun self-care products or parents buying gifts.

What Are You Good At? (Skills Needed)

What talents or knowledge do you already have that will help you make and sell this product?

Example: I like crafting, I've made bath bombs before, and I'm good at decorating things to make them look nice.

What Will You Need? (Materials or Resources)

Make a list of supplies, tools, or other things you'll need to create your product.

Example: I'll need baking soda, essential oils, molds, packaging, and labels.

What Makes It Special? (Unique Selling Point)

What makes your product stand out from others? Why would someone choose your product over another?

Example: My bath bombs are made with natural ingredients and come with a surprise charm inside!

NOTES:

Step One

CHECK IN

Choosing Your Business Idea

You've taken the first big step in starting your own business by exploring what you love, what you're good at, and how those things can become a real business! Use this page to reflect on what you've learned and get ready for what's next.

What Did You Discover?

What are 2 things you love doing?

✏️ _____

✏️ _____

What are 2 things you're really good at?

✏️ _____

✏️ _____

How did you combine your interests and skills to come up with a business idea?

✏️ _____

Your Business Idea

What business idea are you most excited about?

✏️ _____

Are you planning to sell a:

☐ Product ☐ Service ☐ Not sure yet

Why do you think this idea could work for you?

✏️ _____

Reflection Time

What was the hardest part of Step 1?

✏️ _____

What helped you get through it?

✏️ _____

Do you want to:

☐ Move forward with this idea

☐ Brainstorm one more idea before Step 2

You're Ready for Step 2: Build Your Business Plan!

In the next step, you'll start building the plan for your business, including your mission, your product or service, how much to charge, and more.

Take a breath. You've got this. Let's keep going!

NOTES:

STEP TWO:
CREATE A BUSINESS PLAN

Complete Pages 24 - 50

Creating a business plan is like making a map for your business. It helps you stay organized, make smart choices, and explain your idea to others. Let's break it down into easy steps:

Introduction (Executive Summary): The Introduction is a short paragraph about your business idea, commonly referred to as an executive summary.

- What are you selling or offering?
- What problem does it solve, or need does it meet?
- What makes your idea different or special?

Example: I'm starting a dog-walking service for busy pet owners. It helps dogs get the exercise they need when their owners are at work or school.

Product or Service Details: After the Introduction, you will explain exactly what you'll be selling or doing.

- Is it a product? What is it made of?
- Is it a service? What will you do for your customers?

Example: I'll make handmade friendship bracelets using colorful thread and beads. Customers can choose their colors and names for the bracelet.

How It Will Work (Operations & Management): Think about how your business will run every day.

- Will you work alone, have a co-worker, or get help from family or friends?
- How will you keep track of orders, customers, and supplies?
- Will you deliver products, sell at events, or offer your service only at certain times?

Example: I'll take orders through a form and fill them after school each day. My mom will help me buy supplies on weekends.

Your Money Plan (Financials): Figure out the money side of your business:

- How much does it cost to make your product or offer your service?
- How much will you charge customers?
- How much do you think you can earn?

Example: Each bracelet costs me $1 to make, and I'll sell them for $5. If I sell 10 bracelets, I'll earn $50 and spend $10—so my profit is $40.

Your business plan doesn't have to be perfect—it just needs to show your ideas clearly. Once you write it out, you'll be ready to take your next big step as a young entrepreneur!

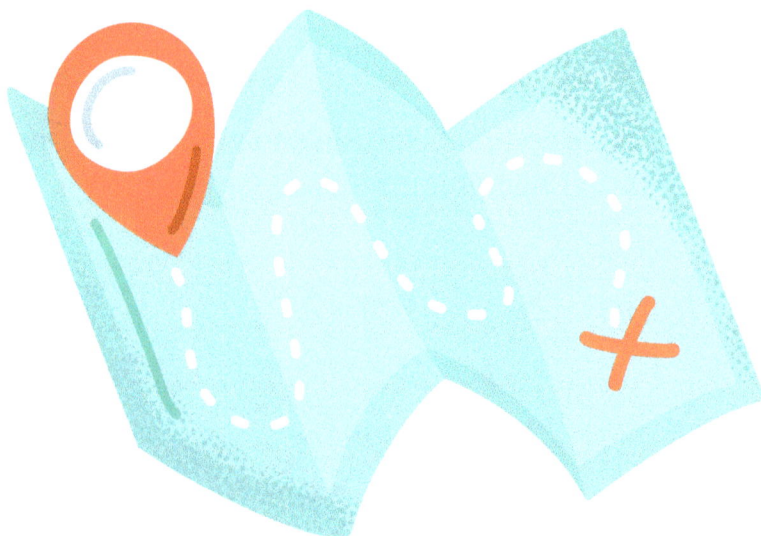

EXAMPLE EXECUTIVE SUMMARY

1. Mission Statement:

My Lemonade Stand is on a mission – solving the big problem of sweltering days without a refreshing drink in hand.

Picture this: the sun's blazing, and you're dreaming of something ice-cold. That's where I step in!

2. What's The Problem I'm Solving?:

- Imagine those scorching summer afternoons when you're desperately searching for something cool and delicious to quench your thirst. That's the issue I'm tackling – the need for the ultimate refreshing beverage!

3. What Is My Solution?:

- I'm introducing the coolest, zestiest lemonade in town. Freshly squeezed lemons, a hint of magic, and a whole lot of smiles – that's my secret recipe. My Lemonade Stand is not just about drinks; it's a full experience of joy in a cup.

4. What Makes My Business Special?:

- What makes my lemonade stand out? It's not just the ingredients; it's the love and care I put into every cup. Plus, my stand isn't just a stand – it's a hub of happiness, with friendly faces and sunny vibes.

5. Why My Business Matters:

- Why is my Lemonade Stand so important? Because it's not just about quenching thirst; it's about creating moments of joy and bringing people together. My lemonade isn't just a drink; it's a mood lifter, a summer memory in a glass, and a reason to smile.

So, join me under the colorful umbrella, grab a cup of sunshine, and turn ordinary days into extraordinary memories together.

Remember, your executive summary is like a movie trailer–it should excite everyone to see the whole thing. Now it's your turn to write your Executive Summary. Have fun!

MY EXECUTIVE SUMMARY

This is your business introduction. Use these five prompts to help you write a simple and powerful summary of your business idea!

My Mission Statement: Why does your business exist? What do you want it to do?

Example: I want to bring smiles and sweet refreshment to my neighborhood with delicious, homemade lemonade.

What Problem Am I Solving? What need or challenge are you helping with?

What Is My Solution? What are you offering to fix that problem or meet that need?

What Makes My Business Special? How is your product or service different or better than others?

Why My Business Matters: Why is your business exciting and important to you and others?

PRODUCT OR SERVICE DESCRIPTION

Think small to dream big. It's better to start with a focused, fun idea rather than overwhelming yourself. Consider offering a limited number of products or services and doing them really well. It's better to do one thing well than 10 things badly. Your customers will appreciate excellence in your product or service. Find your unique niche – that special thing that sets you apart in the market. Creating your niche sets the foundation for building a distinctive brand.

Starting small doesn't mean you can't have big dreams. Think of your business like a seed; as you nurture and grow, there will always be room for growth in the future. Keep it simple and effective; simplicity is powerful and manageable as you learn the entrepreneurial world. Treat your business like a cool science experiment – test ideas, and learn from them. Every challenge is a lesson leading to success.

Describe what you will be selling or offering.

For example, if you're making handmade jewelry, explain the types of jewelry you'll create and the materials you'll use.

OPERATIONS & MANAGEMENT

Use this worksheet to determine what help you might need when running your business.

What Tasks Need to Get Done? (Examples: taking orders, making products, delivering items, keeping track of money).

1.

2.

3.

4.

5.

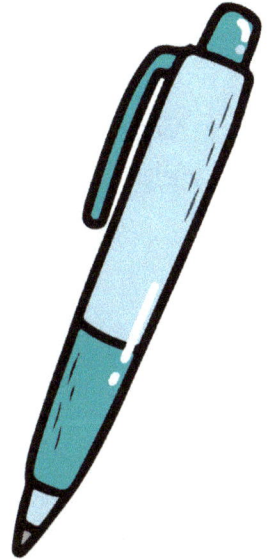

Circle the tasks you feel confident doing on your own.

Put a ⭐ next to the tasks you enjoy doing the most.

Identify the tasks you might need help with or find challenging or hard to do.

1.

2.

3.

4.

HELP! I NEED SOMEONE!

Write down the names of family members, friends, or other trusted individuals who could assist you with those tasks:

Person Who Can Help

Person Who Can Help

Job Assignment

Job Assignment

Determine how often you might need assistance for the tasks you need help with. Will you do the task daily, weekly, monthly, or occasionally (now and then)?

Discuss with your family, friends, or a mentor how you can delegate or share the responsibilities for those tasks.

Remember, running a business is a team effort, and asking for help is okay. By delegating tasks, you can focus on the aspects of the business you enjoy the most and ensure that everything runs smoothly. Working together with others can make your business even more successful.

Keep in mind that as your business grows, your needs may change, and it's important to regularly evaluate your operations and management to ensure efficiency and effectiveness.

Step Two Mid-Point
CHECK IN
Building Your Business Plan

Great job!!! You're halfway through building your business plan! Let's pause to check in with your progress, ideas, and how you're feeling about your new business.

What I've Figured Out So Far:

My business idea is:

✎ _____

I will offer a:

☐ Product ☐ Service ☐ Both

What makes my business special:

✎ _____

Why my business matters:

✎ _____

How My Business Will Work

One thing I've learned about running a business is:

✎ _____

A task I'm confident I can handle:

✎ _____

A task I might need help with:

✎ _____

Someone I could ask for help is:

✎ _____

Quick Reflection

What's been the most exciting part of Step 2 so far?

✏️ _____

What part has been the most confusing or challenging?

✏️ _____

What questions do I still have? (It's okay if you don't have any!)

✏️ _____

Next Up: Let's Talk Money!

 In the next part of Step 2, you'll figure out what to charge, how much things cost, and how to make sure your business is making money—not losing it. You're getting closer to launching something amazing!

WHAT SHOULD I CHARGE?

Let's break down how to figure out the cost of your product or service and set an appropriate price for your business.

Figuring Out the Cost of My Product or Service:

List all the materials or resources you need to create your product or provide your service.

Your materials might include things like ingredients, packaging, or equipment. Figure out the cost of each item on your list. You can do this by looking things up online or by taking a trip to the store!

Add up the costs of all the items to see the total cost of making your product or providing your service.

Setting the Right Price:

Think about the costs you figured out earlier and other things like your time and effort in producing or delivering your product or service.

Think about your target audience. Who will be interested in buying your product or service?

Research what other businesses charge for similar products or services in your town. Researching what other businesses charge will give you an idea of the market price.

Think about your goals and the amount of money you want to make. Do you want to earn spending money or save money to buy something special? Do you want to reinvest in your business? Are you saving for a future goal?

FIGURING OUT WHAT YOU SHOULD CHARGE

Let's say you're starting a small baking business and want to sell homemade cookies. Here's how you can calculate the cost and set a price:

Calculating the Cost of Goods:

First, list the ingredients you need to make and package your cookies:

○ —— FLOUR ——

○ —— SUGAR ——

○ —— BUTTER ——

○ —— CHOCOLATE CHIPS ——

○ —— PACKAGING ——

Now, research the prices for each ingredient and how much it will cost to make and package a batch of cookies. You can research by looking up prices online, checking newspaper advertisements, or visiting the store.

FLOUR - $2.00

SUGAR - $2.00

BUTTER - $4.00

CHOCOLATE CHIPS - 5.00

PACKAGING - $1.00

Once you figure out what your ingredients are going to cost, add them up to figure out what it is going to cost you to bake and package a batch of cookies.

$2 + $2 + $4 + $5 + 1 = $14

So, in this example it costs $14 to make and package a batch of cookies.

Now that you know how much it costs to make a batch of cookies, it's time to figure out how much you should charge for them. Picking the right price is super important.

If you charge too little, you might not make any money, or worse, you could lose money. But if you charge too much, people might not want to buy from you because they can get something similar for less. A smart price is one that helps you make a profit while still being fair and close to what other businesses charge.

Figuring out how much to charge for your cookies:

First, check out what other cookie sellers or local bakeries charge. For example, they might sell cookies for $3 each.

Next, think about your time. If it takes you one hour to bake a batch of 12 cookies, how much do you think your time is worth? You get to decide!

Now, think about profit. Let's say you want to make $10 from every batch you bake. That's your goal after covering all your costs.

Here's an example to help you figure out your cookie price:

Cost to make one batch (ingredients, packaging, etc.): $14
Number of cookies in one batch: 12
How much profit you want to make: $10

Now do the math:

$14 (cost) + $10 (profit) = $24 (total price you need to make per batch)

$24 ÷ 12 cookies = $2 per cookie

So, you would charge $2 for each cookie.

Quick tip:

Pricing is all about balance. You want to make sure you're covering your costs, earning some money, and still keeping the price fair so people want to buy from you. Check your prices every once in a while and make changes if you need to.

COST CHART EXAMPLE

My Costs To Make A Batch Of Cookies	$
Item	Amount
FLOUR	$2.00
SUGAR	$2.00
BUTTER	$4.00
CHOC. CHIPS	$5.00
PACKAGING	$1.00
MY TIME / DESIRED PROFIT	$10.00
TOTAL COST	$24.00
AMOUNT OF PRODUCT (UNITS)THIS MAKES	12
TOTAL COST / AMOUNT OF PRODUCT (UNITS) $24.00 / 12	SELLING PRICE $2.00

Review and update your pricing periodically as your business evolves and market conditions change. Pricing depends on your business goals, brand positioning, and customer perception.

COST CHART

My Costs To Make A Batch Of Cookies	$
Item	Amount
TOTAL COST	
AMOUNT OF PRODUCT (UNITS)THIS MAKES	
TOTAL COST / AMOUNT OF PRODUCT (UNITS) $ /	SELLING PRICE

TRACKING INCOME AND EXPENSES

First
WRITE DOWN YOUR INCOME

Income is the money your business earns when someone buys your product or pays for your service.

For example, if you sell cookies for $2 each and you sell 10 cookies, your income is:

$2 x 10 = $20

Write down all the money you make from selling your product or service. Add it up and put the total in the "Income" section of your budget.

INCOME		
DATE	WHERE THE MONEY CAME FROM	AMOUNT

Second
LIST YOUR EXPENSES

Expenses are things you spend money on to run your business.

These can include:

Ingredients or supplies to make your product
Tools or equipment to provide your service
Flyers, signs, or other ways to tell people about your business (marketing!)
Even money you want to save for a future business goal

There are two types of expenses:

Fixed expenses stay the same each month (like a booth rental or website fee)

Variable expenses can change (like buying more supplies when you get more orders)

Write down what you spend money on and how much it usually costs. Add everything up and put the totals into your budget under Fixed and Variable Expenses.

FIXED EXPENSES

DATE	SOURCE	AMOUNT

VARIABLE EXPENSES

DATE	SOURCE	AMOUNT

Third
FIGURE OUT YOUR PROFIT

How much money did you make? To figure out your profit, subtract your total expenses (both fixed and variable) from your income (the money you earned).

Here's the formula: Income – Expenses = Profit

If your profit is a positive number, awesome! That means you made more money than you spent. You can choose to save it, spend it, or invest it back into your business.

If your profit is a negative number (you spent more than you made), it's time to look at your budget and find ways to lower your costs or make more sales.

Forth
CHECK-IN AND MAKE CHANGES

Running a business means checking your numbers often. Take a look at your budget from time to time to see how you are doing.

Are you spending too much?

Is your profit more than you expected?

Is your profit growing or are you starting to make less money every month?

If something isn't working, that's okay—just adjust your budget, pricing, or goals to help your business do better.

Tracking your money helps you make smart choices and reach your goals faster!

Remember!
Budgeting is all about managing your money wisely. It's important to save, spend responsibly, and plan for the future. By filling out a budget, you can become more aware of your money and make smarter financial choices.

MONTHLY BUDGET

MONTH OF: _____

INCOME

DATE	INCOME SOURCE	AMOUNT

FIXED EXPENSES

DATE	SOURCE	AMOUNT

VARIABLE EXPENSES

DATE	SOURCE	AMOUNT

BUDGET SUMMARY

SOURCE	AMOUNT
INCOME	
FIXED EXPENSES	
VARIABLE EXPENSES	
BALANCE = REVENUE / PROFIT	

EXPENSE TRACKER

MONTH:

YEAR:

DATE	DESCRIPTION	AMOUNT	BALANCE
		TOTAL:	

NOTES:

INCOME TRACKER

MONTH OF: _____ YEAR: _____

	DESCRIPTION	SOURCE	AMOUNT
1			
2			
3			
4			
5			
6			
7			
8			
9			
10			
11			
12			
13			
14			
15			
16			
17			
18			
19			
20			
21			

What is a business plan, and why do you need one?

CREATING A BUSINESS PLAN

A business plan is like a guide that helps you plan out your business step by step.

It helps you think about important things like:

- What you're going to sell
- Who your customers will be
- How much money you'll make
- How you'll let people know about your business

Think of it like getting ready for a big trip, you wouldn't leave without knowing where you're going, how you'll get there, or what to bring. Your business plan does the same thing for your business. It helps you stay on track and be ready for anything that comes your way.

A business plan also helps you explain your idea to others, like adults who might want to help you, customers who want to know more, or even someone who might invest in your business.

And guess what? Your business plan doesn't have to be perfect the first time. You can change it and make it better as your business grows. That's all part of learning and being a real entrepreneur!

Wait until you complete your Marketing Plan before you fill in the items marked with a ⚡.

BUSINESS PLAN

⚡ COMPANY NAME: _____

PRODUCTS & SERVICES OFFERED:

SUPPLIES, EQUIPMENT & RESOURCES NEEDED:

TELL PEOPLE ABOUT THE PRODUCTS OR SERVICES YOU ARE SELLING:

_____

_____

_____

_____

THE PROBLEM MY COMPANY SOLVES:

⚡ MY POTENTIAL CUSTOMERS ARE:

HOW CUSTOMERS BENEFIT FROM MY PRODUCTS & SERVICES:

⚡ MY MARKETING PLAN

_____

_____

_____

_____

HOW MY PRODUCTS & SERVICES ARE DIFFERENT FROM OTHERS ALREADY BEING SOLD BY OTHERS:

HOW MY PRODUCTS & SERVICES ARE SIMILAR TO OTHERS ALREADY BEING SOLD BY OTHERS:

THE SKILLS, KNOWLEDGE, AND RESOURCES I HAVE THAT WILL HELP MY BUSINESS:

_____

_____

_____

_____

_____

_____

_____

THE FINANCIALS

AMOUNT I PLAN TO SELL EACH PRODUCT FOR:

COST TO MAKE EACH PRODUCT:

PROFIT PER PRODUCT/SERVICE SOLD:

MY COMPANY'S BREAK EVEN POINT
(THE POINT WHERE YOU DON'T LOSE MONEY)

BUSINESS START UP COSTS:

PROFIT PER PRODUCT / SERVICE:

NUMBER OF SOLD PRODUCTS / SERVICES
NEEDED TO BREAK EVEN:

Step Two
⋇CHECK IN⋇
Building Your Business Plan

You're officially building your business like a real CEO! In Step 2, you took your awesome idea and began putting together a real plan. Use this check-in page to reflect on what you've learned and how far you've come.

Your Executive Summary

What is your business mission (in your own words)?

✏️ _____

✏️ _____

What problem are you solving and how?

✏️ _____

Operations & Management

List 2 important tasks your business will need to do regularly:

✏️ _____

✏️ _____

What tasks are you good at?

✏️ _____

Who can help you with the tasks you might need help with?

✏️ _____

Pricing & Budgeting

What are you selling (product or service)?

✏️ _____

How much will you charge?

$ _____

Why did you choose this price?

✏ _____

Money Matters

What is income?

✏ _____

What is an expense?

✏ _____

Why is it important to track income and expenses?

✏ _____

Your Business Plan

How do you feel about your business plan so far?

☐ I feel great! ☐ I'm still figuring some things out ☐ I might want to change a few things

What part of Step 2 did you enjoy the most?

✏ _____

What part was the hardest?

✏ _____

Ready for Step 3: Creating a Marketing Plan

Now that you've built a strong foundation, it's time to get the word out! In Step 3, you'll learn how to reach your perfect customers and tell the world how awesome your business is. Get ready to market like a pro!

STEP THREE: CREATE A MARKETING PLAN

Complete Pages 57 - 79

How to Tell People About Your Business (Marketing!)

Once you have a great business idea, it's time to spread the word and get customers! Great marketing makes your product stand out and makes people want to buy what you are selling!

That's where your marketing plan comes in. Let's break it down:

1. Who Are You Selling To? (Your Target Audience)

Think about who would be most excited to buy what you're offering. That's your target audience.

- If you're pet-sitting, your audience might be pet owners who travel a lot.
- If you're selling cool bracelets, your audience might be kids your age or parents shopping for gifts.

2. What Do You Know About Them?

Do a little research. Are other people already selling something similar? What makes your idea different or better? This helps you understand your market and stand out!

3. What Makes You Special?

This is your unique selling point—what makes your business awesome and different from others.

- Maybe your jewelry is made from recycled materials.
- Maybe you include handwritten thank-you notes with every order.
- Think about what would make someone want to choose YOU.

5. Set a Marketing Budget

You don't need a ton of money to market your business. Figure out how much you can spend and use it wisely.

- You might print flyers, make a free website, or use free social media tools.

6. What's Working (and What's Not)?

Keep track of what brings in customers. Are more people finding you on Instagram? Are your flyers helping?

If something isn't working, it's okay to try something new!

Bonus Tip: Ask for Help!

Running a business is a big adventure! You'll learn along the way, and it's okay to make mistakes. If you ever feel stuck, ask a parent, teacher, or trusted adult for advice. Most of all, have fun and be proud of yourself for building something amazing!

Who are you selling your product or service to?

IDENTIFYING YOUR TARGET AUDIENCE

Figuring out who your product or service is for is a big part of running a successful business. This is called your target audience—the group of people most likely to buy from you.

Let's walk through some fun steps to help you understand who your customers are and why they'll be excited about what you're selling. Complete the worksheet on page 57 to figure out your perfect customer. When you know your audience, you can create something they'll love—and that helps your business grow!

Know What You're Selling

Before you can run a business, you need to really understand your product or service.

Ask yourself:
- What am I offering?
- What makes it cool, helpful, or fun?
- How does it solve a problem or make someone's life easier?

Keep your answer simple and easy to explain. If you can tell a friend what you sell in one sentence, you're on the right track!

Imagine Your Perfect Customer

Now think about who would love what you're selling. This is called your target audience. To make it easier, create a pretend customer!

Give them a name and answer these questions:

How old are they?
Are they a boy, a girl, or either?
What do they do for fun?
Where do they live or shop?
Why would they be excited to buy from you?

Example: Emma is 13, loves animals, and likes cute accessories. She would love handmade pet collars with charms.

What Do They Like?

Once you have your ideal customer in mind, think about what they like, need, or want. You can learn more by:

- Asking your friends or family what they would buy
- Watching what's popular at school or online
- Doing a quick poll or survey

The better you understand your customer, the easier it is to create something they'll want to buy—and keep coming back for!

Check Out Other Businesses

Take a look at other businesses that sell something like you do.

- What do they do really well?
- What do their customers like about them?
- How is your idea different or better?
-

Now think about why your product or service would be a better choice for your customers. What makes it more fun, more helpful, or more exciting?

What Makes You Stand Out?

Every great business has something special about it—this is called your unique value. Ask yourself:

- What do I offer that others don't?
- How does my business make life better or more fun for people?

Then write a short sentence that tells people why they should pick your business.

Example: "I make custom keychains with your name on them so you can show off your style everywhere you go!"

By doing these steps, you'll understand your customers better, and you'll be ready to show them why your business is awesome. Remember: being different is a good thing, and your ideas matter. Have fun sharing what makes your business shine!

MY PERFECT CUSTOMER

A "persona" is creating an imaginary person. When we talk about a "customer persona," it means constructing a kind of imaginary person who could be interested in what you're selling – giving them a name and age and defining what makes them tick. It's a way to understand better who might be interested in what you're offering. So, it's essentially like crafting a virtual friend to help you get into the minds of your potential customers!

Let's create a persona for a stylish and socially conscious young adult who appreciates quality refreshments at your lemonade stand!

Example Persona: Meet Monique!

Let's say you have a stylish lemonade stand. Who would love it? Let's imagine someone who would be your biggest fan.

Name: Monique
Age: 22

Background:
Monique is a college student who loves fashion, art, and cool places to hang out. She cares about the planet and likes to support small businesses that do good things.

Interests:
Monique enjoys going to fun cafes, shopping for stylish clothes, visiting art shows, and trying new, tasty drinks. She also loves snapping cute pictures to share with her friends online.

Needs and Wants:
She's looking for drinks that taste great and also look really cool. She wants her purchases to match her style and be good for the environment. She likes when a product makes her feel happy and unique.

Online Presence:
Monique spends a lot of time on Instagram and TikTok. She follows creative pages, shares fun photos, and likes finding new places and products to post about.

Communication Style:
Monique likes brands that are fun, friendly, and creative. She pays attention to bright colors, cool designs, and simple, positive messages.

Shopping Behavior:
She likes to buy things that are unique and worth the price. She'll spend a little more on something if it's cute, eco-friendly, or helps a local business. She likes to explore and find new favorites.

Goals:
Monique wants to enjoy life, stay stylish, and support good causes. She wants products that help her feel good and express who she is.

How Your Lemonade Stand Can Attact Monique As a Customer:

- Offer fun flavors with a cool look—like colorful cups or fruit garnishes
- Use eco-friendly straws, napkins, or packaging
- Decorate your stand with a stylish theme (think pastel colors, fun signs, flowers)
- Post photos on social media and use hashtags she'd like
- Smile, be friendly, and make your lemonade stand a place people want to visit and share!

IMAGING MY PERFECT CUSTOMER

Let's create your perfect customer, someone who would be super excited to buy your product or service! Use this worksheet to imagine what they're like, what they care about, and how you can connect with them

My Perfect Customer:

Name: _____

What would you like to call your ideal customer? Example: Monique, Max, Jordan

Age: _____

How old are they? Example: 14, 25, 62

What's Their Life Like?

Write a few sentences about your customer. Are they in school? Do they have hobbies? What do they do during the day? Example: Max is a 13-year-old middle schooler who loves playing video games and drawing cartoons. He's always looking for cool things to share with his friends.

What Do They Like? (Interests)

(Think about what your customer enjoys doing or learning about.)
Example: Sports, music, fashion, pets, tech, reading

What Do They Need or Want?

What are they looking for? What problem does your product or service help solve?
Example: They want snacks that are healthy and tasty, or they need a fun gift for a friend's birthday.

How Do They Spend Time Online?

Are they on YouTube, TikTok, Instagram? Do they shop online? Watch videos?
 Example: Max watches DIY videos on YouTube and scrolls funny memes on Instagram.

How Do They Like to Communicate?

Do they prefer short videos, cool pictures, funny messages, or in-person talks?
Example: Max loves colorful posts with emojis and quick, funny videos that explain things fast.

Why Would They Love Your Business?

What makes your product or service perfect for your ideal customer? Example: Max would love my sticker packs because they're funny, one-of-a-kind, and he can use them to decorate his sketchbook.

How Do They Shop? (Shopping Behavior)

Where and how do they like to buy things? Do they shop online or in stores? Do they like cool packaging, fun displays, or fast service? Example: They like to buy things that look cool, are easy to get, and feel like something special. They like shopping at school markets or from fun stands.

What Are Their Goals or Hopes?

What do they care about or want? Are they looking for fun, style, convenience, or something helpful? Example: They want to have fun with their friends, try new things, or show off something unique.

How Can My Business Attract Someone Like _____?

Use your perfect customer's name here! What can you do to make your business exciting to them? Example: I can design my packaging to be colorful and cool, make my product fun to share, and offer quick service with a smile.

Imagine Your Business Through Their Eyes

Now that you know your ideal customer, picture what your business looks like to them.
- What would catch their attention?
- What would make them want to stop and shop?
- How can you make their experience fun, easy, or exciting?

Your job is to make your business feel like it was made just for them!

Fantasy Product Challenge
MARKET TO YOUR HERO!

Materials:

- Paper or a notebook
- Pens, pencils, crayons, or markers
- A big imagination!

Step 1: Pick a Fictional Character

Think of a character you love from a book, movie, video game, or TV show. This could be a superhero, a wizard, a cartoon animal—anyone!

Examples: Elsa, Spider-Man, SpongeBob, Eleven, Percy Jackson, Mario

Step 2: Invent a Product Just for Them

Now think: What cool product would that character totally love?
 It can be something magical, high-tech, silly, or helpful. Design a product that fits into their world. Draw it if you'd like!

Examples:

- A heat-proof hairbrush for Elsa
- A silent web shooter for Spider-Man
- A bubble-powered scooter for SpongeBob

Step 3: Match the Product to Their Needs

Think about your character's life:

- What do they want or need?
- What are their challenges or hobbies?
- How could your product make their life easier or more fun?

Example for Elsa:

- She's often cold and alone—maybe she needs a magical hoodie that keeps her warm and sings lullabies!

Write a few sentences or make a list connecting your product to your character's needs.

Step 4: Plan How You'll Sell It (Marketing Plan)

Now it's time to figure out how you'll get your character excited about your product! Use these questions to help you build your plan:

Product Description

Write a short and fun description of your product.

What does it do? Why is it awesome? Why would your character want it?

Design and Packaging

What does your product look like? Draw it or describe it.

Think about colors, shapes, logos, or packaging that would grab your character's attention.

How Will You Promote It?

How will you tell your character about your product?
Would they see it in a commercial? A flyer? A cool video?

Think of creative ways to get their attention!

Pricing

How much will your product cost?

Make sure it's a fair price based on what it does and what your character could afford in their world.

Write down the price and explain why it's a good deal.

Step 5: Show Off Your Idea

Time to bring your plan to life! You can:

- Make a poster
- Act out a skit or commercial
- Design a slide show
- Record a video

Use props, drawings, music, or anything else that makes your presentation fun and eye-catching. Team up with a friend or family member if you want!

Step 6: Share Your Plan!

Get ready to perform or present your idea. Show it to your family, class, or mentor. Tell them why your product is perfect for your character and use your best persuasive language to sell it!

Smile, be confident, and most of all—have fun. You're learning how to speak to your audience, just like real business owners do!

Bonus Challenge: Create a Slogan!

Write a short, catchy slogan to advertise your product. Make it fun and memorable!

Example: "Stay warm like a queen – with the Chill-Proof Cloak!"

Check Out A Real Business!
BUSINESS SCAVENGER HUNT

Business Name:

OPEN

Pick a business in your town or neighborhood, maybe a restaurant or store, and answer the questions below to help you learn what works well and what could be better. This will help you get ideas for your own business!

What's Working Well?

- What are the best parts of this business?

- What do they do that makes customers happy?

What Could Be Better?

- What are some things they could improve or fix?

- If you owned this business, what would you change?

What Can You Learn From Them?

- What ideas or lessons could you use for your own business?

- What did you like that you might want to copy or do differently?

About Their Product or Service:

- Is what they sell unique or special in some way?

- Would you want to buy from them? Why or why not?

Customer Service:

- What are some things they could improve or fix?

- If you owned this business, what would you change?

Advertising and Marketing:

- How do they let people know about their business?

- Do they have signs, ads, social media, or other ways to get attention?

Prices:

- Are the prices too high, too low, or just right for what they offer?

- Would kids or adults be willing to pay?

Store Appearance:

- Is the store or shop clean and neat?

- Do the employees look tidy and professional?

Organization:

- Is the store easy to walk around and find things?

- Is everything in the right place?

Location:

- Is it in a good spot where lots of people can find it easily?

Your Overall Thoughts:

- What's your overall opinion of this business?

- Would you go back or recommend it to someone?

BUSINESS REVIEW

Business Name:

	Excellent	Good	Neutral	Bad	Very bad
Is their product or service special or different?	○	○	○	○	○
Are the employees friendly and helpful?	○	○	○	○	○
What do you think about their marketing and advertising?	○	○	○	○	○
What do you think about their prices?	○	○	○	○	○
Is the store clean? Do the employees look tidy?	○	○	○	○	○
Is the store well organized?	○	○	○	○	○
Is the store located in a good location? Is it easy to get to?	○	○	○	○	○

Please provide any additional feedback.

HOW CAN YOU APPLY WHAT YOU LEARNED FROM REVIEWING THIS BUSINESS TO YOUR OWN BUSINESS?

Build Your Brand
CREATE A MOOD BOARD

This activity will help you bring your business idea to life through colors, pictures, and creativity! You'll make a mood board to show the look and feel of your brand.

WHAT YOU'LL NEED:

- Poster board or corkboard
- Magazines or printed images from the internet
- Scissors and glue sticks
- Markers or pens
- Extras: stickers, ribbon, glitter, washi tape—anything fun!

WHAT'S A MOOD BOARD?

A mood board is like a collage that shows the vibe of your business. It helps you decide:

- What your brand should look like
- What feelings or ideas your business gives off
- What colors, styles, or words match your business best

STEP 1: THINK ABOUT YOUR BUSINESS

Before you start cutting and gluing, ask yourself:

- What kind of business am I creating?
- What colors or styles match my product or service?
- How do I want people to feel when they see my business? (Excited? Calm? Confident?)
- What kind of customers do I want to attract?

STEP 2: GATHER YOUR IMAGES

Flip through magazines or search online for images, words, and symbols that match your brand idea. Look for:

- Colors and fonts you like
- Pictures that show your business's style
- Words or phrases that describe your brand (fun, fast, cool, caring, etc.)

Cut them out and get them ready to arrange!

STEP 3: DESIGN YOUR MOOD BOARD

Start laying out your images on the board. Move things around until it feels just right. Add:

- Your business name (if you have one!)
- Doodles, notes, or sketches with markers
- Stickers or other fun decorations

Make it colorful and unique—just like your business!

STEP 4: REFLECT AND SHARE

Once your mood board is finished, take a step back and look at it. Ask yourself:

- Does this show what I want my business to be?
- Do the colors, words, and images match my brand idea?
- Would this attract the kind of customers I imagined?

Then, share your board with a friend, classmate, or mentor. Explain your theme and how you made your choices. Ask for feedback!

BONUS: WHAT'S NEXT?

Use your mood board to help design:

- A logo
- A website or social media profile
- Your product packaging
- Ads or flyers

This is the first step in bringing your brand to life!

Hi! My name is...
NAME YOUR BUSINESS

Let's come up with a cool name and logo for your business. These two things are a big part of your brand— they help people remember you and recognize what you're all about!

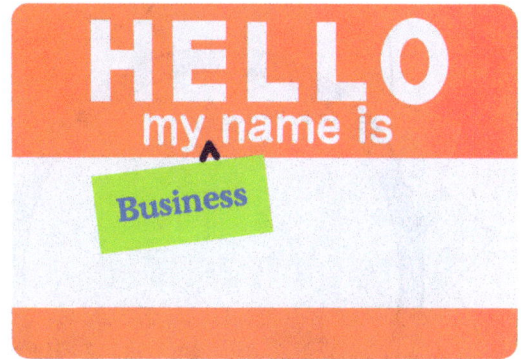

HELLO
my name is
Business

Step 1: Brainstorm a Business Name

Start by thinking of words that describe:

- What your business sells
- What makes it special
- How you want people to feel when they see it

Then try these tricks:

- Mix two words together
- Use rhymes or fun sounds (like "Cool Cakes" or "Bubble Bliss")
- Use your name or initials (like "Ava's Art" or "J&M Treats")

Quick Challenge:

Set a timer for 5 minutes and write down as many name ideas as you can—no idea is too silly! Let your imagination run wild.

Step 2: Pick Your Favorites

Look at your list. Which names:

- Are easy to say?
- Are fun or catchy?
- Make sense for your product or service?

Top 3 Challenge: Use the worksheet on the next page!

Pick your favorite 3 names and ask your friends, family, or teacher which ones they like best. Get feedback! Also, don't forget to do some research to make sure no one else is already using your name for a similar business.

MY TOP THREE NAME CHOICES

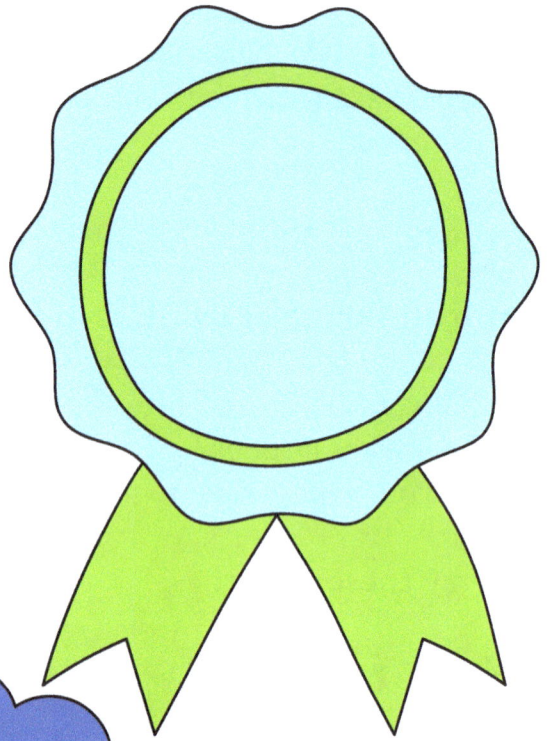

THE WINNING BUSINESS NAME IS......

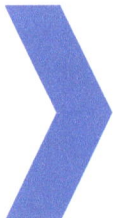

DESIGNING A LOGO

Your logo is a small picture or design that represents your business. It should show off your personality and give people a quick idea of what your business is all about. Let's create one that really stands out!

Step 1: Start Sketching

Grab some paper and start drawing rough ideas for your logo.

Think about:
- Symbols or shapes that match your business (like stars, hearts, animals, tools, etc.)
- Words or letters that show your business name
- Fonts (fancy, bold, playful?) that match your style

Step 2: Pick Your Colors

Think about what colors represent your business and what your customers might like.

- Bright colors = fun and playful
- Dark colors = serious or professional
- Pastels = calm and creative

Choose colors that feel like you and fit your business vibe.

Step 3: Try It Digitally

Once you have an idea you like, try creating your logo using a computer! You can use free tools like Canva to build a cool, polished version of your design. It lets you play with fonts, colors, shapes, and images—and even create a whole brand look!

Step 4: Use Your Mood Board!

Look back at your Mood Board and use it to guide you as you design your logo!

MY LOGO IDEAS

MARKING PLAN

What's My Brand?

Think of your brand as your business's personality. What kind of vibe or message do you want people to feel when they see your business?

Three words to describe my brand:
(Fun? Fancy? Friendly? Creative? Cool?)

My brand colors and style:
(Bright? Pastel? Bold? Sporty?)

My logo looks like:
(Describe it if you haven't drawn it yet)

Who Am I Talking To? (My Audience)

Let's get specific about who you want to reach. You've already thought about this a little—now we'll zoom in!

My perfect customer is...

Age:

What they love:

Where they hang out (online or in person):

Why do they care about my business?

What Makes Me Stand Out?

This is your marketing message—the big reason someone should be excited about what you're offering.

My product/service is awesome because...

Here's what makes it different from what others offer:

When people hear about my business, I want them to feel...

How Will People Find Me? (Promotion Plan)

This is all about spreading the word!

Check all the ways you plan to tell people about your business:

☐ Posters/flyers
☐ School announcements
☐ Social media (with adult help)
☐ Word of mouth
☐ Business cards or stickers
☐ Local events or pop-ups
☐ Website or online shop

Other ideas:

Now write your plan: "To get the word out, I will…"

What Do I Want to Happen? (Marketing Goals)

Time to dream big (but realistic)!

I want to sell _____ items this month.

I want _____ new people to find out about my business.

I want to get _____ followers or likes on my page.

I want to be invited to participate in a _____ (event, market, etc.).

My Marketing Calendar

Pick 2–3 things to do each week to promote your business.

Week	What I'll Do to Promote My Business
1	
2	
3	
4	
5	
6	
7	
8	
9	
10	

Step Three

CHECK IN

Marketing Like A Boss

Wow! You should be so proud of yourself for wrapping up step three! You figured out who your perfect customers are, created a brand style that's all your own, and even built your marketing plan. Take a moment to reflect on what you've learned before we jump into the next exciting step.

Who Am I Selling To?

My perfect customer is someone who:

_____

One thing I learned from the "Market to a Hero" activity is:

_____

One cool thing I noticed during the business scavenger hunt:

_____

My Brand Vibe

My brand mood board includes these words, colors, or ideas:

_____

My business name is:

_____

I designed a logo that includes:

_____

Final Thoughts on Marketing

Something I learned about marketing that surprised me:

✏️

_____

Something I want to keep working on is:

✏️

_____

I feel (circle one):

Confident   Still Thinking   A Little Stuck   Super Excited

✅ Don't Forget!

Go back to the end of Step 2: Create a Business Plan and finish filling out your business plan now that your marketing plan is complete. You're getting closer and closer to launching something amazing!

Next Up: Guppy Tank!

Now it's time to take everything you've worked on and present your business! In Step 4, you'll get to share your ideas, show off your logo and brand, and present your business plan just like a real entrepreneur. Get ready to shine in the Guppy Tank!

NOTES:

STEP FOUR:
GUPPY TANK

It's your time to shine! In this activity, you'll present your business idea to a group of "investors" (that could be parents, teachers, friends, or classmates). This is your chance to show off your plan, explain why it's awesome, and practice your presentation skills!

First
CREATE A VISUAL AID

Create a visually appealing and informative poster or slide deck to showcase your business during the "Guppy Tank" presentation.

What to Include in Your Presentation:

1. Business Name & Logo

Start by showing off your business name and your cool logo. Make it clear, fun, and easy to remember.

2. What's Your Business About?

Give a quick intro.

- What are you selling or offering?
- What makes it different or special?
- Why should people care?

3. Who's It For? (Target Market)

Talk about your ideal customers:

- How old are they?
- What do they like?
- Why would they want to buy your product or service?

4. What Are You Selling?

Describe your product or service:

- What is it?
- What problem does it solve?
- How will it make someone's life better, easier, or more fun?

5. How Will You Tell People About It? (Marketing Plan)

- Will you make posters, post on social media, or talk to friends and family?
- How will people learn about your business?

6. Let's Talk Money (Financials)

You don't need to be a math expert! Just share the basics:
- How much does it cost to start?
- How much will you charge?
- How do you plan to make a profit?

7. Meet the Team

- Who's working on this business?
- Are you doing it solo or with friends or siblings?
- Tell us a little about you!

Second
PRACTICE YOUR PITCH LIKE A PRO!

Now that you've created your slide deck or poster, it's time to get ready to present your business like a boss!

Rehearse Out Loud

- Say it out loud—don't just read it in your head.
- Stand up, use hand gestures, and pretend you're on stage.
- Practice in front of a mirror, a family member, or a friend. Ask them for feedback!

The more you practice, the more confident you'll feel.

Use Your Visual Aids

Got a poster? Slides? A sample of your product? Use them while you practice! Show them off while you talk so they help tell your story.

Tips:

- Make sure everything is easy to read
- Don't put too many words on one page or slide
- Point to your visuals when they connect with what you're saying

Time Yourself

Try to keep your presentation between 5 and 10 minutes.

Use a timer to:

- Make sure you don't talk too fast or too slow
- Leave room for questions at the end
- Know where to trim if it's running long
- If you're over time, shorten parts that aren't as important—or combine a few points together!

Third
PRESENT LIKE A BOSS

It's showtime! Here's how to rock your Guppy Tank presentation:

- Speak clearly and confidently
- Make eye contact with your audience
- Use your hands to help explain things
- Smile! Let your excitement show!

Be ready to answer questions or explain anything your "investors" are curious about. You've done the work—now it's your time to shine!

Remember:

The goal is to show off your awesome idea and convince your audience that your business is worth supporting.

Ask for what you want!

- Do you want a loan to start your business?
- Would you like help getting customers?
- Want them to buy a piece of your company or give you advice?

Speak up and make your ask!

DID YOU KNOW...
J.K. ROWLING WAS REJECTED BY 12 PUBLISHERS BEFORE SOMEONE FINALLY SAID YES TO HARRY POTTER AND THE SORCERER'S STONE? SHE DIDN'T GIVE UP—AND NEITHER SHOULD YOU.

Step Four

CHECK IN
Guppy Tank Wrap-Up

You did it! You stood up, shared your business idea, and made your pitch like a real entrepreneur. Let's take a moment to look back on everything you accomplished and get ready for the final step—bringing your business to life at a Pop-Up Shop!

My Presentation

What I used as a visual aid:

_____

One thing I was proud of during my presentation:

_____

One thing I want to improve next time:

_____

What I Asked the Investors For
(✔ Check all that apply or write your own!)
□ A loan to help start my business
□ Help selling my product or service
□ Customers to try what I offer
□ Advice or ideas
□ Something else: _____

What I Learned

One thing I learned about presenting my business idea:

_____

One question the investors asked me:

_____

Something I want to do differently or better next time:

✏️ _____

Next Up: Pop-Up Shop!

 Now that you've pitched your business, it's time to take it out into the real world. In Step 5, you'll learn how to set up a booth, talk to real customers, and start selling your product or service.

Get excited! Your first pop-up shop is coming soon!

STEP FIVE:
POP-UP SHOP

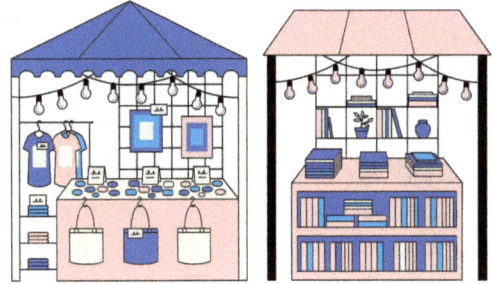

PREPARING FOR A POP-UP SHOP

A pop-up shop is a fun way to show off your business, sell your products or services, and meet real customers face-to-face. Let's get you ready to shine!

Step 1: Get Your Products or Services Ready

- Make sure your items look great! Are they clean, neat, and ready to sell?
- If you're offering a service (like face painting or gift wrapping), practice ahead of time so you're confident and ready.
- Bring any supplies you'll need, like bags, signs, or handouts.

Step 2: Set Up a Great Display

- Make your table or booth eye-catching and fun. Use signs, bright colors, or props to grab attention.
- Arrange your items in a way that's easy to see and shop.
- Offer samples or small demos to show off what you do!

Step 3: Decide on Your Prices

- Choose fair prices that match the value of what you're offering.
- Use price tags or make a sign so customers can easily see how much things cost.
- Set up a way to take payment—like cash, a parent's phone with a payment app, or a change box with small bills and coins.

Step 4: Spread the Word

- Let people know about your pop-up shop ahead of time!
- Post on social media with help from an adult, and ask your friends and family to share.
- Make a flyer or ask your school if you can tell your classmates.

Step 5: Talk to Your Customers

- Smile and say hello when people come by. Be friendly and helpful.
- Tell them about your product or service—what it is, how it works, and why it's awesome.
- Be ready to answer questions and explain what makes your business special.

Step 6: Keep Track of Sales & Feedback

Use a simple sheet to write down what you sell and how much you earn. This helps you see what people liked the most, and what to do better next time.
Ask customers what they liked and if they have any suggestions. Their feedback can help you grow!

Bonus Tip: Find a Place to Set Up

You can ask:

- A local shop if they'll host you for an afternoon
- A craft fair or farmers market if they have spots for young entrepreneurs
- Your school or library if you can set up a table during an event

Most Important: Have Fun!

Running your own pop-up shop is an amazing experience. Be proud of what you've created and enjoy meeting new people. You're building something awesome—good luck!

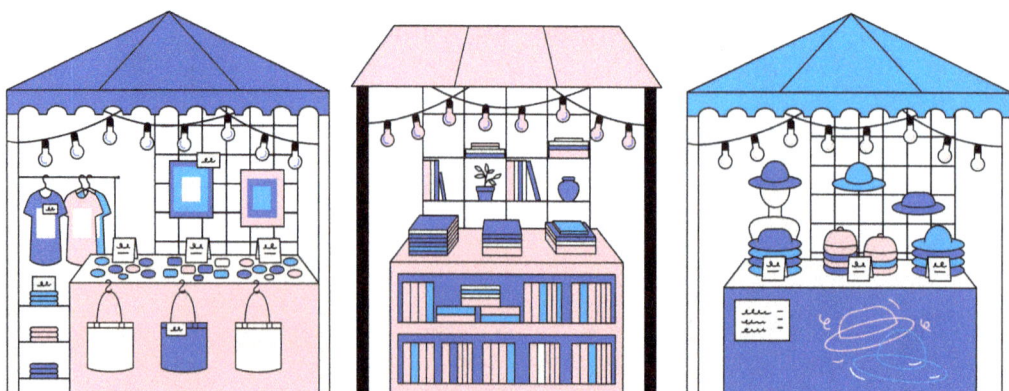

CUSTOMER SERVICE 101

What is customer service?

Customer service means being kind, helpful, and respectful to the people who buy or use your product or service. It's about making sure your customers feel welcome, listened to, and appreciated.

When you treat customers well, they're more likely to come back—and even tell their friends about your business!

Imagine This:

You have a lemonade stand. Someone walks up, and you greet them with a big smile and say, "Hi there! How's your day going?"

That's customer service!

Now they ask,"What flavors do you have?"

You take the time to explain each one, help them decide, and say thank you when they buy.

That's great customer service, too!

Why Does It Matter?

- Happy customers are more likely to buy from you again
- They'll tell friends and family about your business
- You'll build a reputation for being helpful, respectful, and awesome to work with
- It helps your business grow and succeed

Remember:

Customer service is not just about selling, It's about making people feel important and cared for.

No matter what kind of business you have (a lemonade stand, dog walking, jewelry-making, or anything else), great customer service will help you stand out.

SALES TRACKER

Month :   **Year :**

Order #	Date	Item sold	Sale price	Your Cost	Fees	Revenue

CUSTOMER FEEDBACK

Thank You for your purchase! Your opinion is important, and we would love to know what you love and what you think we can do better.

How satisfied were you with the product/service you received?

♡ Unsatisfactory ♡ Satisfactory ♡ Good ♡ Very Good ♡ Excellent

Did the product/service meet your expectations?

♡ Unsatisfactory ♡ Satisfactory ♡ Good ♡ Very Good ♡ Excellent

How was our customer service?

♡ Unsatisfactory ♡ Satisfactory ♡ Good ♡ Very Good ♡ Excellent

How likely are you to recommend our product/service to others?

1 2 3 4 5 6 7 8 9 10

Not likely   Most likely

Any comments or suggestions?

_____

_____

_____

Step Five

CHECK IN

Pop-Up Shop Wrap-Up

You did it! You stood up, shared your business idea, and made your pitch like a real entrepreneur. Let's take a moment to look back on everything you accomplished and get ready for the final step—bringing your business to life at a Pop-Up Shop!

My Pop-Up Prep

My product or service was:

_____

One thing I did to make my booth stand out:

_____

Something I remembered to bring that helped a lot:

_____

Sales & Prices

How much did I charge for my product or service?

_____

Did I make any money? How much?

_____

Was there anything I sold out of or wish I had more of?

_____

Talking to Customers

What did I say to customers when they came to my booth?

✎ _____

One thing I felt confident doing:

✎ _____

One thing I want to get better at:

✎ _____

Customer Feedback

What did people like about my business?

✎ _____

Did anyone give me a suggestion for next time?

✎ _____

One change I'd like to try in the future:

✎ _____

You're a Real Entrepreneur!

You've taken your idea all the way from a brainstorm to a real-life business. That's a huge accomplishment—be proud of yourself! Keep using what you've learned, and who knows? This might be just the beginning.

BUSINESS TERMS MADE EASY

Assets

Assets are things you own that are worth something.

Examples:
- Money in your wallet
- A bike, gaming system, or a collection of trading cards

If you could sell it or trade it because it has value, it's an asset!

Liabilities

Liabilities are things you owe to someone else.

Examples:
- You borrowed $5 from a friend
- You promised to pay your sibling back for a snack they bought you

If you have to pay someone back, that's a liability.

Why It Matters:

Knowing the difference between assets and liabilities helps you make smart money choices.

Assets = help you grow your money
Liabilities = money you need to repay

Revenue

Revenue is the money your business earns from selling something.

Example: If you sell lemonade for $1 a cup and sell 10 cups, your revenue is $10.

It's not the same as profit—it's just the total money coming in before you subtract costs.

Entrepreneur

An entrepreneur is someone who starts and runs their own business. They come up with an idea, take a chance, and work hard to make it successful—even if it means taking some risks.

Example: If you create a slime shop, pet-sitting business, or make and sell bracelets, you're an entrepreneur!

Budget

A budget is a plan for your money.

It helps you decide:

- How much money you have
- What you'll spend it on (needs and wants)
- What you want to save for

It's like a roadmap that helps you make smart choices with your cash.

Supply and Demand

This is how much of a product you have (supply) and how much people want it (demand).

Example:

- If you only have 5 cupcakes but 10 people want one, demand is high.
- If you bake 30 cupcakes and only 3 people want them, you made too many!

Finding the right balance helps your business succeed.

Brand

Your brand is what makes your business stand out.

It includes your:

- Name
- Logo
- Colors and style
- Personality

A strong brand helps people remember you and know what your business is all about.

Cash Flow

Cash flow is the money moving in and out of your business.

- Money coming in from sales = good cash flow
- Money going out for supplies, rent, or other costs = expenses

Positive cash flow means you're making more than you're spending!

Business Plan

A business plan is a written guide that explains:

- What your business does
- Who your customers are
- How you'll make money
- What your goals are

It helps you stay organized and show others (like investors or partners) how your business will work.

YOU DID IT
WAY TO GO, CEO!

You just did something amazing; you've started your own business! As your business grows, keep dreaming big, learning new things, and improving your skills. Here are a few things you might think about doing as your business grows in the future:

1. Make Your Business Official (LLC)

When you're older and your business gets bigger, you can register it as something called an LLC (Limited Liability Company). This means your personal money and stuff (like your phone, bike, or savings) are protected if something goes wrong in your business. Grown-up business owners do this all the time!

2. Get a Business Tax ID Number

A Tax ID Number is like a special code that tells the government your business exists. You'd need this if your business gets big enough to pay taxes (that's what adults call income taxes). It's kind of like your business's own ID card.

3. Open a Business Bank Account

As your business grows, it's smart to keep your business money separate from your personal money. Opening a bank account just for your business helps you stay organized and makes it easier to track how much you're earning and spending.

4. Get Business Insurance

Even small businesses can face surprises! Business insurance helps protect your stuff (like supplies or equipment) and can cover you if something unexpected happens. It's like a safety net for your business.

5. Build Your Online Presence

Having a website or social media page is a great way to tell people about your business, especially as you grow.

- You can share updates, photos, or product info
- People can find you more easily online
- You could even start selling your products through an online store someday!

CERTIFICATE

OF COMPLETION

proudly presented to

in recognition of their successful completion of the

THE YOUNG ENTREPRENEUR ACADEMY

This certificate is awarded in recognition of the creativity, hard work, and entrepreneurial spirit demonstrated throughout the program.

From developing a business idea to presenting a pitch and running a pop-up shop, this achievement shows commitment, growth, and an exciting step toward future success.

We are proud to celebrate your accomplishments!

L. Brickley

LAINA BRICKLEY

The Young Entrepreneur Academy

NOTES:

NOTES:

NOTES:

NOTES:

About The Author

Laina J. Brickley, a native of Northeast Ohio, is a multi-faceted professional passionate about empowering communities through entrepreneurship. Armed with a Juris Doctorate from the University of Toledo, a Master of Public Health from the Medical College of Ohio, and a certificate in Leadership Principles from Harvard Business School, Laina brings diverse skills to her roles.

With over a decade of experience in wealth management, Laina transitioned her career to the non-profit sector, leaving an indelible mark as a vital force at Habitat for Humanity. She later went on to serve as the dynamic President & CEO of the St. Landry Chamber of Commerce in Louisiana, where she was committed to fostering economic growth and innovation within the community.

Laina's inspiration for "The Young Entrepreneur Academy" stems from her role as a mother to Carter and Ava, her two remarkable children, who were the muse behind the development of The Young Entrepreneur Academy program and its very first graduates. Their enthusiasm for learning and creating fueled the vision of a program that empowers young minds to dream, innovate, and lead.

Laina cherishes family moments outside her professional commitments with her husband, Andrew. An avid reader and an enthusiastic traveler, Laina is driven by a passion for lifelong learning and a commitment to building a brighter future for generations to come. "The Young Entrepreneur Academy" is a testament to her dedication to shaping young minds and fostering a culture of innovation and leadership.